100 Interactive Riddles and Brain Teasers

The Best Short Riddles and BrainTeasers with Clues
for Stretching and Entertaining your Mind

Puzzleland

D1167215

Table of Contents

About Puzzleland

We make innovative puzzle books.

Our mission is to create amazing reading experiences that elevate your mind to a higher level of thinking.

You can explore our products at

http://www.amazon.com/author/puzzleland

Thank you for purchasing this book and don't forget to leave a review* on Amazon!

*Visit   trk.as/vw9e   to easily leave your review!

Introduction

100 Interactive Riddles and Brain Teasers is a great fun book for teens and adults who look for some creative ways to spend their free time, entertain their mind or simply keep themselves busy while waiting in public locations!

100 popular short riddles and brain teasers have been compiled in this book. This collection contains some of the world's most famous riddles, and also many lesser known gems. For each one of the 100 riddles a clue is provided to help you find the solution!

Challenge yourself, your friends, partner or family and have some fun exercising your brain at the same time!

Why Interactive?

The original bestselling *100 Interactive Riddles and Brain Teasers* was first published as a kindle book specially formatted for digital devices (such as Kindle, Fire, PC etc.)

In its digital version, the book can provide clues - simply with a click - before providing the answer! This means that you can see a clue before seeing the answer - which is a great "interactive" feature, that makes the book a lot more fun!

We decided to make this book available also in a printed version for the readers that would love to buy a printed copy for their library.

Clues and Answers

In the printed version, clues and answers can be found at the back of each page. To see the clue, look at the back of the page, top left. To see the answer, look at the back of the page, bottom right.

Difficulty Level

The difficulty level of the riddles is appropriate for beginner teens or adults, and even for smart kids.

Order the Kindle Version

If you wish to order the original kindle version of *100 Interactive Riddles and Brain Teasers*, visit 9nl.org/mky2

Feel free to send us your feedback and ideas for improvement at puzzlelandbooks@gmail.com.

Let's get started!

PUZZLELAND

Riddles #1-15

PUZZLELAND

1

The Four Children

Mary's mother has four children. The first child is named April. The second child is named June. The third child is named May. What is the fourth's child's name?

Clue!
The
fourth
child
is
not
named
after
a
month.

Answer:
Mary
is
the
fourth
child
of
course!

2

Mt.Everest

Before Mt. Everest was discovered, what was the highest mountain in the world?

Clue!
The
highest
mountain
in the world
and the
highest
mountain
known
to the world
are not
the
same
thing.

Answer:
Everest!
It
just
wasn't
discovered
yet!

4

3

No Questions Asked

What doesn't ask questions but needs to be answered?

Clue!
Every
house
has
one!

Answer:
A
telephone!

A Shorter Word

What word becomes shorter when you add two letters to it?

Clue!
This
word
is
a
short
one,
too.

Answer:
Short
becomes
shorter
when
you
add
two
letters!

8

5

Odd Addition

What is the answer to this addition?

1 + 1 + 1 + 1 + 1

1 + 1 + 1 + 1 + 1

1 + 1 x 0 + 1 = ?

Clue!
All
numbers
you can see
belong in
one equation.
These numbers
can all be
written
in 1 line
instead of
3.

Answer:
The answer is 30.
There are two tricks
in this question.
The first is 1 times 0.
This is only a distraction.
Yes, 1 times 0 is 0, but that
doesn't affect anything else
in the equation.
The second trick is
that the lines ending with 1
don't have a + sign next to them.
That means they should be combined
with the following line.
Here are the numbers, all on one line:
$1 + 1 + 1 + 1 + 11 + 1 + 1 + 1 + 11 + 1 \times 0 + 1 = ?$
And the answer to that equation is 30.

6

Anna's Birthday

Anna was born on December 24th, yet her birthday always falls in the summer. How is this possible?

Clue!
Where
on
earth
Decembers
are
as
hot
as
summers?

Answer:
Anna
lives
in
the
southern
hemisphere.

7

So Fragile!

What is so fragile that when you say its name you break it?

Clue!
It
will
be
broken
as
soon
as
you
start
saying
any
word.

Answer:
Silence.

A Single Stroke

How can you alter the following equation by a single stroke (straight line) to make it correct?

5 + 5 + 5 = 550

Clue!
Focus
on
the
plus
sign.

Answer:
Add
a
diagonal
line
on the
top left
of the
first
plus
sign
to convert
+ into a 4.

16

The Riddle of Eugene

Eugene died after a long life of 87 years, but on his headstone the following epitaph was written:

"Eugene lived a good long life - He loved his sons and pretty wife - He was kind, generous and deserved nothing but praise - Even if he only had 21 birthdays."

How is this possible?

Clue!
Eugene
was born
on a very
special
day,
which
gives
the
answer
to the
problem.

Answer:
Eugene
was born
on
February 29th
in a
leap year.
Consequently,
in his 87 years,
he only
witnessed
twenty-one
of his
actual birthdays.
The other years
there was
no February 29th.

18

10

The Thirsty Horse

A horse is tied to a 20 foot long rope. The horse wants to get some water that is 30 feet away. The horse gets the water easily. How is this possible?

Clue!
Every
rope
has
two
sides.

Answer:
The
other
side
of
the
rope
isn't
tied
to
anything!

11

If You Share Me

If you have me, you want to share me. If you share me, you haven't got me anymore. What am I?

Clue!
You
share
it
by
using
your
mouth.

Answer:
A
secret.

12

The Words' Party

You watch a group of words going to a party. They are outside the club and a word either enters through one of two doors or is turned away by the doorman. 'HIM' goes through door number 1 and 'BUG' goes through door number 2. 'HER' is turned away. 'MINT' and 'WAVE' go in through door 1, 'DOOR' and 'CORD' take door 2 and 'THIS' and 'That' are not allowed in.

What determines whether a word can enter and which door they must use?

Clue!
The key
is in
the
curve.

Answer:
Door number 1
is for words composed of
capital letters
written using only
straight lines,
such as A, E, F, H, and I.
(Therefore only the letters
AEFHIKLMNTVWXYZ
are allowed through door 1).
Door number 2 is for words
with capital letters
that have a curve
(BCDGJOPQRSU).
Words that are composed of
both straight
and curved letters
(or lowercase letters)
are not allowed in.
The word 'THAT'
would have been sent
through door number one,
if the letters
had been capitalized.

13

Once in a Minute

What occurs once in a minute, twice in a moment and not once in a thousand years?

Clue!
Look
for
the
answer
inside
the
question.

14

Find the Number

What is the highest regular counting number that is spelled without the use of the letter "N"?

Clue!
2
digits
of
this
number
are
the
same.

Answer:
Eighty-eight.
From
then
on,
they
all
have
the
letter
"N".

15

Up and Down

What goes up and down but never, never moves?

Clue!
It
helps
you
go
up
and
down,
also.

Answer:
A
staircase.

Riddles #16-30

16

A Crime Paradox

This is the only crime that is not punishable if committed. What is it?

Clue!
The
victim
and
the
criminal
are
always
found
in
the
same
building.

Answer:
Suicide

34

17

Don't Give me Water

Give me food and I will live. Give me water and I will die. What am I?

Clue!
It
is
friendly
when
you
are
close
but
it
will
bite
you
if
you
touch
it.

Answer:
Fire.

18

The Bathtub Challenge

We fill up a bathtub with water. If you had a teaspoon, a teacup and a bucket, what would you do to empty the bathtub as fast as possible?

Clue!
Really,
what
would
you
do
if
you
were
in
your
own
bathroom?

Answer:
Pull
out
the
plug,
of course!

19

Acronyms

What do these represent?

24 = HiaD
26 = LotA
7 = DotW
9 = LoaC
12 = SotZ

Clue!
The
words
are
acronyms.
The
first
one
is
24 "hours in a day".

Answer:

24 hours in a day

26 letters of the alphabet

7 days of the week

9 lives of a cat

12 signs of the Zodiac

20

Cats and Mice

5 cats can catch 5 mice in 5 minutes. How many cats does it take to catch 100 mice in 100 minutes?

Clue!
Make
the
best
of
what
you've
got!

Answer:
5 cats.
The
same
five
could
keep
catching
5 mice
every
5 minutes
for
100 minutes.

21

Slice my Head

You use a knife to slice my head and weep beside me when I am dead. What am I?

Clue!
The
crime
was
committed
in
the
kitchen.

Answer:
An
onion.

22

Lighter than a feather

I'm lighter than a feather, yet the strongest man can't hold me for much more than two minutes. What am I?

Clue!
It's
as
light
as
air.

Answer:
His
breath.

23

Before Breakfast

What are two things people never eat before breakfast?

Clue!
If
you
skip
breakfast,
what
can
you
eat?

Answer:
Lunch
and
supper.

48

24

Mothers & Daughters

Two mothers and two daughters were making cakes. Each one of them made one cake, yet in the end only three cakes were made. How is this possible?

Clue!
All
women
belong
in
the
same
family.

Answer:
A
girl,
her
mother
and
her
grandmother
were
making
the
cakes!

25

In a Chess Club

Two men in a chess club were playing chess. They played five games. Each man won the same number of games. How is this possible?

Clue!
These
two
men
were
not
the
only
ones
playing
chess
in
the
chess
club
that
day.

Answer:
They
played
different
people.

26

A Long Word

What one word has all 26 different letters in it?

Clue!
Even
first
graders
know
this!

Answer:
The
Alphabet.

27

Oranges and Bags

How can you put 21 oranges in 4 bags and still have an odd number of oranges in each bag?

Clue!
The
trick
is to
use
one
of the
bags
in a
different
way.

Answer:
Put
seven
oranges
in each
of the
first
three
bags
and then
put
these
three
bags
inside
the
fourth
bag.

56

28

Two Teachers

Two teachers teach at the same school. One is the father of the other's son. What relation are they to each other?

Clue!
They
all
live
in
the
same
house,
too!

Answer:
Husband
and
wife.

29

A Not so Empty Pocket

How can a pants pocket be empty and still have something in it?

Clue!
This
"something"
might
be
the
reason
why
the
pocket
is
empty.

Answer:
A
hole.

30

A Rare Year

In what year did Christmas Day and New Year's Day fall in the same year?

Clue!
Take
a
look
at
a
calendar
to
check
if
this
will
happen
this
year.

Answer:
It
happens
every
year,
on
the
1st
of January
and
25th
of December.

Riddles #31-45

31

Me and My Twin Brother

I am pronounced as one letter, but written with three. Me and my twin brother are blue, brown or green. What am I?

Clue!
Everyone
has
a
pair
of
them.

Answer:
Eye.

32

A Man in the Rain

A man walked outside in a heavy rainstorm for twenty minutes without getting a single hair of his head wet. He didn't wear a hat, carry an umbrella, or hold anything over his head. His clothes got soaking wet. How could this happen?

Clue!
Think,
what
type
of
hair
can't
the
rain
mess
up?

Answer:
The
man
has
no
hair,
he
is
bald.

33

White and Dirty

What is black when it is clean and white when it is dirty?

Clue!
Teachers
use
it.

Answer:
A
Blackboard.

34

Greater than God

What is greater than God, more evil than the devil, the poor have it, the rich need it, and if you eat it, you'll die?

Clue!
It's
the
opposite
of
all.

Answer:
Nothing.

35

I Have Hands

I have hands but can not clap. I can not speak but I can answer one question. What am I?

Clue!
Some
times
this
is
the
only
thing
you
might
hear
in
the
silence
of a
room.

Answer:
A
clock.

36 *Reading*

What does this represent?

| R | E | A | D | I | N | G |

Clue!
Combine
the
word
and
the
lines.

Answer:
"Reading
between
the
lines."

37

It Never Lasts Forever

You always want it. Sometimes you can have it and be at it,

but it never lasts forever. What is it?

Clue!
Its
opposite
brings
death
and
destruction.

38

How Many Times

How many times can you subtract the number 5 from 20?

Clue!
The
answer
is
not
"4 times."

Answer:
Only
once,
after
that
you
will
be
subtracting
5
from
15,
then
5
from
10
....

39

The Wedding Paradox

He has married many women, but has never been married. Who is he?

Clue!
We
always
wears
black.

Answer:
A
preacher.

40

No Legs

What has a head, a tail, is brown, and has no legs?

Clue!
You
might
have
one
in
your
pocket
right
now.

Answer:
A
penny.

41

Penguins' Eggs

Even if they are starving, natives living in the Arctic
will never eat a penguin's egg. Why not?

Clue!
It's
because
they
haven't
seen
any
penguins
lately.
Do
you
know
why?

Answer:
Penguins
live
in
Antarctica,
not
in
the
Arctic.

42

Six Letter Word

I'm a word, six letters long, I sometimes enter with a gong.

All in order from A to Z, I start with the letter B.

What is the word?

Clue!
All
start
with
this
word.
Even
the
old
testament!

Answer:
Begins.
(Usually,
when a show
or meditation
begins
they
sound
the
gong.
Also,
the letters
are in alphabetical order.
And,
the first words
of the old testament
are
"In the beginning
there was light...")

88

43

One Eye

I have one eye, but I can not see. I am so small that you can easily lose me. What am I?

Clue!
Once
a
god
said
that
a
camel
could
go
through
it.

Answer:
A needle.
Once
Jesus said,
"Again I tell you,
it is easier
for a camel
to go through
the eye
of a needle
than for
someone
who is rich
to enter
the kingdom
of
God."

90

Kids and Apples

A basket contains 5 apples. Do you know how to divide them among 5 kids so that each one has an apple and one apple stays in the basket?

Clue!
The
fifth
kid
thought
that
the
basket
would
be
a
nice
gift
for
his
mother.

Answer:
4 kids
get an
apple
(one apple
for each one of them)
and the fifth kid
gets an apple
with the basket
still containing
the apple.

92

45

Scratch my Head

Take one out and scratch my head, I am now black but once was red.

Clue!
It
should
be
kept
out
of
reach
of
children.

Answer:
A
match.

Riddles #46-60

46

Not Twins

Recently a mother gave birth to two girls on the same day, at the same time, in the same month and year and yet they're not twins. How is this possible?

Clue!
The
two
girls
have
a
brother
who
is
not
older
than
his
sisters.

Answer:
The
two
girls
are
two
of
a
set
of
triplets.

98

47

Cities without Houses

Where do you find roads without vehicles, forests without trees, and cities without houses?

Clue!
How
can
you
hold
the
world
in
your
hands?

Answer:
On
a
map!

48

Two Backbones

I have only two backbones and thousands of ribs. I go around the world without moving. What am I?

Clue!
It's
an
invention
that
connects
cities
and
countries.

Answer:
Railroad.

49

Empty Hands

What can you fill with empty hands?

Clue!
It's
something
you
wear.

Answer:
Gloves.

50

A Heavy Word

From what heavy seven-letter word can you take away two letters and have eight left?

Clue!
"Eight"
left;
not
eight
letters!

Answer:
Freight
or
weights!

106

51

Full of Holes

What's full of holes but still holds water?

Clue!
You
have
at
least
one
in
your
bathroom.

Answer:
A
sponge.

52

The Green House

A blue house is made of blue bricks. A yellow house is made of yellow bricks. A red house is made of red bricks. An orange house is made of orange bricks. What would a green house be made of, if not green bricks?

Clue!
What
is
a
"green house"?

Answer:
Glass.

110

53

Never Eaten

What is put on a table and cut but never eaten?

Clue!
They
belong
to
a
family
of
52
members.

54

Before Keeping it

You can't keep this until you have given it. What is it?

Clue!
You
give
it
by
using
your
mouth.

Answer:
A
promise.

55

Your Friends Use it

What is yours but your friends use it more than you do?

Clue!
It
is
not
an
object
and
it
was
given
to
you
when
you
were
born.

Answer:
Your
name.

56

Paradox of a Question

What question can you never honestly answer "yes" to?

Clue!
This
is
a
question
that
roommates,
couples
or
siblings
ask
each
other
often.

Answer:
"Are
you
asleep?"

57

The Three Rooms

A murderer is condemned to death. He has to choose between three rooms. The first is full of raging fires, the second is full of assassins with loaded guns, and the third is full of lions that haven't eaten in 3 years. Which room is safest for him?

Clue!
What
is
more
dangerous:
fire,
an assassin
or a beast
that
has
starved
to death?

Answer:
The
third
room
is
safe!
Lions
that
haven't
eaten
in
three
years
are
dead!

58

The T-days

Can you name four days of the week that start with the letter T?

Clue!
Right
now,
two
of
those
days
are
close,
VERY
close.

Answer:
Tuesday,
Thursday,
Today
and
Tomorrow.

122

59

A Fly in the Tea

A woman was horrified to find a fly in her tea. The waiter took her cup, went into the kitchen and returned with another cup of tea. The woman had a sip from the fresh tea and immediately she shouted, "You brought me the same tea!" How did she know?

Clue!
The
woman
did
not
add
sugar
to
the
second
cup
before
tasting
it.

Answer:
She had
already
put
sugar
in the
first cup
and when
she
tasted
the
new
tea
it was
already
sweet.

60

Sunshine Forecast

It's midnight and it's raining. According to weather statistics, what are the chances of the sun shining in 72 hours from now?

Clue!
What
is
the
reason
why
there
is
no
sun
shining
right
now?

Answer:
72
hours
later
it
will
be
midnight
again,
so
no
sunshine!

126

Riddles #61-75

61

The First Planet

Which was the first planet discovered?

Clue!
The
one
closest
to
you.

62

A Pair of Socks

Inside your sock drawer there are 6 green socks, 4 blue socks, 8 black socks, and 2 red socks. If it's dark and you can't see the colors, how many socks would you have to pull out to be sure you had a matching pair?

Clue!
Imagine
that
each
time
you pull out
a sock,
that sock
is a
different color
than
the previous
sock you
pulled out.

Answer:
You
have
to pull out
five socks.
There are
only
four colors,
so five socks
guarantee
that
two will
be the
same
color.

63

Two Men in a Desert

Two men are in a desert. They both have packs on. One of the guys is dead. The guy who is alive has his pack open, the guy who is dead has his pack closed. What is in the pack?

Clue!
The
dead
man's
last
words
were
"omg
it
isn't
opening!"

Answer:
Parachute.

64
An Ancient Crime

According to an ancient book, a crime of one man caused the elimination of 25% of the world population. Which crime was that?

Clue!
That
ancient
book
was the
Book of
Genesis.

Answer:
When
Abel
was
murdered
by
his
brother
Cain.
Abel
and
Cain
were
the
2 sons
of Adam
and Eve!
So the
population
was reduced
from 4 to 3!

65

Not a Man, Nor a Door

I have no voice and yet I speak to you. I have leaves but I am not a tree.I have a spine and hinges but I am not a man or a door. What am I?

Clue!
It's
not
a
tree
but
its
leaves
are
made
of
tree.

Answer:
A
book.

66

On a Cold Day

You are taking a walk through the park on a cold day, when you notice some objects on the ground: A scarf, a carrot and a few small pieces of coal. Who did these belong to?

Clue!
It's
the
middle
of
January
and
nearly
a
foot
of
snow
fell
last
week.

Answer:
These
items
belonged
to
a
snowman
that
melt!

67

A Great Word

There is a word in the English language in which the first two letters signify a male, the first three letters signify a female, the first four signify a great man, and the whole word, a great woman. What is the word?

Clue!
What
do
you
call
a
man
or
woman
who
has
done
a
very
brave
act?

Answer:
The
word
is
heroine.

68 *Never Arrives*

What is always coming but never arrives?

Clue!
We
are
waiting
for
it
every
day.

Answer:
Tomorrow.

144

69

How Did He See Her?

A man was driving his truck. His lights were not on. The moon was not out. Up ahead, a woman was crossing the street. How did he see her?

Clue!
Why
wasn't
the
moon
out?

Answer:
It
was
a
bright
and
sunny
day!

146

70

Mystery of the Night

They come out at night without being called, and are lost in the day without being stolen. What are they?

Clue!
There
is
not
a
down-to-earth
answer
to
this
question.

Answer:
Stars.

71

Two Insects

It is an insect, and the first part of its name is the name of another insect. What is it?

Clue!
One
of
those
insects,
produces
something
that
humans
eat.

Answer:
Beetle.

72

Playing for Money

Five men sat down to play. They played all night till break of day. They played for money and not for fun. When they had come to square accounts, all had made equal amounts. And no one lost, how all could gain?

Clue!
These
men
did
not
play
games.
What
did
they
play?

Answer:
These
men
were
musicians.

73

Crossing the Creek

A man needs to cross a creek. There is a boat he can take. But, the boat can only take one thing at a time. The man has 3 things he must take. A fox, a sheep, and cabbage. If he were to take the fox, then the sheep would eat the cabbage. But, if he were to take the cabbage, then the fox would eat the sheep. How does the man take the items across?

Clue!
The man
can cross
the creek
with
the boat,
as many
times
he wants.

Answer:
The man
takes the sheep first
(the fox will not eat cabbage.)
The man then returns
and takes the fox
to other side,
but takes the sheep back
to the original side.
He leaves the sheep
and takes the cabbage
to the other side.
Then returns
to the original side
to take the sheep
again to the other side.

154

74

After Today

Where is the only place that yesterday always follows today?

Clue!
This
place
can
be
found
in
a
library.

Answer:
In
a
dictionary!

75

A 30-Foot Ladder

Is it possible to jump from a 30-foot ladder onto concrete without getting hurt?

Clue!
What
do
you
do
if
you
know
that
the
higher
you
are,
the
more
you
will
get
hurt?

Answer:
You
can
jump
from
the
bottom
rung!

158

Riddles #76-90

76

The Man in the Elevator

A man lives on the fifteenth floor of an apartment building. Every morning he takes the elevator down to the lobby and leaves the building. In the evening, he gets into the elevator, and, if there is someone else in the elevator, he goes back to his floor directly. Otherwise, he goes to the tenth floor and walks up five flights of stairs to his apartment. Why does he do this?

Clue!
It has
to
do
with
a problem
he has
with
the
elevator
buttons.

Answer:
The man
is a
dwarf.
He can't
reach
the
upper
elevator
buttons,
but he can ask
people
to push them
for him.

77

The Biggest Words

What two words contain thousands of letters?

Clue!
The
mailman
knows
the
answer!

Answer:
Post office.

78

Bad Luck

When is it bad luck to meet a white cat?

Clue!
Think
of
someone
who
hates
white
cats
as
much
as
black
cats.

Answer:
When
you
are
a
mouse!

166

79

What a Sinner Desires

It may only be given, not taken or bought. What the sinner desires, but the saint does not. What is it?

Clue!
You
can't
have
this
without
having
regrets
first.

Answer:
Forgiveness.

168

80

Birthday Cake

It's your birthday and you have 7 guests. How can you divide a birthday cake into eight equal pieces with only three straight cuts?

Clue!
Think
in
three
dimensions.

Answer:
Make
an X cut
to divide
the cake
into
4 quarters
(two cuts.)
Then
slice
the cake
horizontally
(third cut.)

170

81

The Accident

A family is on a bus. They are all very hungry, and when they spot a diner, they press the stop button. They are the only ones whom went off the bus. One hour later they watch the news and they find out that the bus they were on, crushed from a boulder which fell from a mountain and half of the passengers died. As shocked as they are, the mother said "I wish we never got off." The father could not believe what she had just said, before he said, "Oh, right." Why would the mother say this?

Clue!
What
did the
woman
think
that
made
her
feel
guilty
for what
happened?

Answer:
If they
didn't get off,
the bus
never
would
have stopped,
and would
have been
slightly
further up
the road
when
the
boulder fell.

82

The Doctor's Son

A boy and his father are driving down a road and they run into a tree. The father died instantly and the boy is rushed to the hospital. There, the doctor comes in and says "Oh my god - that's my son!"

How is this possible?

Clue!
The
doctor
is
closely
related
to
the
man
that
died.

Answer:
The
doctor
is
the
boy's
mother.

174

83

Six Glasses

Six glasses are in a row. The first three are full of wine and the second three are empty. With one move only, can you arrange them so empty and full glasses alternate?

Clue!
Think
out of
the box!
You can
also
move
the content
of a glass
instead
of the glass.

Answer:
Pour
the
wine
from
the
second
glass
into
the
fifth
glass.

176

84

Rarely Taken

What is it that everyone requires, everyone gives, everyone asks and that very few take?

Clue!
You
can
have
it
for
free
or
you
can
pay
for
it.

Answer:
Advice.

178

85

In a Dungeon

A man is imprisoned in a dungeon. High up on one of the walls is an unbarred window but it is too high for him to reach, so the man abandons hope of escaping through it. He decides to dig his way out, instead. However hours later he stops as he realises that it would take his entire lifetime to tunnel out. A few days later, an idea comes to his mind, and he begins to dig again. Can you guess what his plan is?

Clue!
His
plan
has
to
do
with
the
unbarred
window.

Answer:
He
wants
to pile up
the dirt
from his
tunneling
and
step on it
so as
to be able
to reach
the
unbarred
window.

180

86

A Puddle of Water

A man was found dead. The detectives found the victim hanging and a puddle of water underneath him. How did the man die?

Clue!
The
murderer
had
placed
something
under
the
man's
feet.
What
was
it?

Answer:
The
man
was
standing
on
ice
that
melted.

182

87

The Miraculous Power

They can bring back the dead. They can make you cry or make you laugh or make you young again. They are born in an instant yet last a life time. What are they?

Clue!
They
live
only
in
our
mind.

184

88

You Have One

You have one, a person has two, a gorilla has three and a human being has four, a personality has five and a citizen of this world has six. What am I?

Clue!
Its
body
is
made
of
letters.

Answer:
Syllable.

89

Eighty Eight Keys

I have 88 keys that can't open any door. What am I?

Clue!
Touch
it
and
it
sings.

Answer:
A
piano.

188

90

Around the Yard

What runs around the yard without moving?

Clue!
It
keeps
the
house
safe.

Answer:
A
fence.

Riddles #91-100

91

Not in the Sky

I'm the part of the bird that's not in the sky. I can swim in the ocean and yet remain dry. What am I?

Clue!
Imagine
a bird
flying
above
you.
What
part
of
the
bird
is
not
in
the
air?

Answer:
Shadow.

92

The Cassette Recorder

A man was found dead with a gun in his hand. A cassette recorder was found on his desk, next to him. The detective pressed the play button on the tape recorder and he heard: "I can't go on. I have nothing in this world to live for." Then there was the sound of a gunshot. The detective immediately said that it was murder and not suicide. How did he know?

Clue!
It is
so obvious,
that
the detective
did not need
to rewind
the tape
to listen
to the
message
again!

Answer:
The cassette
had started
at the
beginning
of the
message,
so
someone else
rewinded
the tape
and
then
left
the
room.

93

The More you Take

The more you take the more you leave behind. What are they?

Clue!
Imagine
yourself
walking
on
a
beach.

Answer:
Footsteps.

94

Animals of the Ark

How many of each type of animal did Moses take on the Ark?

Clue!
First,
ask
yourself:
When did
he build
the ark,
before
or after
releasing
the Jews
from
slavery?

Answer:
None,
it
was
Noah
that
built
the
ark!

95

A Simple Division

Divide 10 by 1/2 and add ten. What is the answer?

Clue!
It's
not
15.

Answer:
10: 1/2 = 20.
20 plus 10 = 30.
The
answer
is
30.

96

Going to St.Ives

As I was going to St. Ives, I met a man with seven wives.

Each wife had nine sacks. Each sack had nine cats. Each cat had five kits.

Kits, cats, sacks and wives, how many were going to St. Ives?

Clue!
There
is
a
distraction
in
this
riddle.

Answer:
Only
I
was
going
to
St. Ives.

97

Two Tourists in India

A man and a woman were on vacation in India. They walked into a restaurant and the waiter brought them both beverages. The beverages were the same. The man drank his glass down right away, and nothing bad happens to him. The woman took her time, drinking slowly. She got sick one hour later. Why?

Clue!
They
both
had
a
glass
of
ice
lemonade.

Answer:
The
ice cubes
were made
from
contaminated
water.
The man
drank it down
before
the ice
had
a chance
to melt.

206

98

Coin in the Bottle

Put a coin into an empty bottle and insert a cork into the neck. How can you remove the coin without removing the cork or breaking the bottle?

Clue!
What
goes
up,
can
go
down.

Answer:
Push
the
cork
down
into
the
bottle.
Then
shake
the
coin
out.

99

Timepieces

A sundial has the fewest moving parts of any timepiece. Which has the most?

Clue!
It's
one
of
the
most
ancient
time-measuring
devices,
too.

Answer:
An
hourglass.
It
contains
thousands
of
grains
of
sand.

210

100

Sun and Dragon

There is a man stuck in a room with 2 doors. In those two doors are the following:

In the 1st, a sun that will toast anyone that enters.

In the 2nd, a fire breathing dragon that smites anyone in the room.

How does the man escape?

Clue!
A
better
question
would
be...
"when
does
the
man
escape?"

Answer:
He
waits
until
nightfall
and
goes
out
the
1st
door.

212

Congratulations!

If you have made it to here, congratulations!

We hope you enjoyed these riddles.

Leaving a review for this book will encourage us to create more books like this one. It doesn't have to be a long review, as a matter of fact even a one-word review would also be helpful for us.

Follow this link to easily post your review in less than a minute:

trk.as/vw9e

Thank you for supporting our products!

Puzzleland

Check out our other puzzle books at

http://www.amazon.com/author/puzzleland

Made in the USA
Lexington, KY
26 October 2018